Little Book of
FROGS

BY: EMILY ATKINSON

Little Book of Frogs

Copyright © 2023 by Emily Atkinson

ISBN: 9798378638796

Independently Published

Graphics from Canva

My name is Whitney and I am a White's tree frog.

I live in the forests of Australia and southern New Guinea. I can also be found in towns around homes. It is warm and moist where I stay.

I can be many different colors. I can be light blue, purple, gray, or green. My color can even change depending on what mood I am in and what is around me.

I like to eat all kinds of insects.

I am one of the biggest tree frogs
and can get up to 4 ½ inches.

I am sometimes called a dumpy frog because I can get big folds of fat on my body and above my eyes.

I have large, sticky pads on my toes that help me to hold on to things. This makes me a very good climber.
Can you climb like me?

My name is Bonnie. I am an African bullfrog.

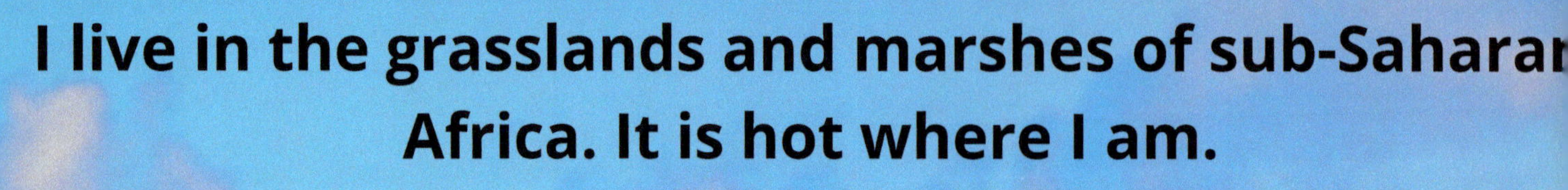

I live in the grasslands and marshes of sub-Saharan Africa. It is hot where I am.

I like to live in puddles and ponds. When it gets too dry, I bury myself in the ground and wait for it to rain again. I can stay buried for almost a whole year!

I am light brown, green and yellow.

I will eat almost anything that is smaller than I am, which is a lot of things! I can eat small mammals, other frogs, birds, insects, and some reptiles.

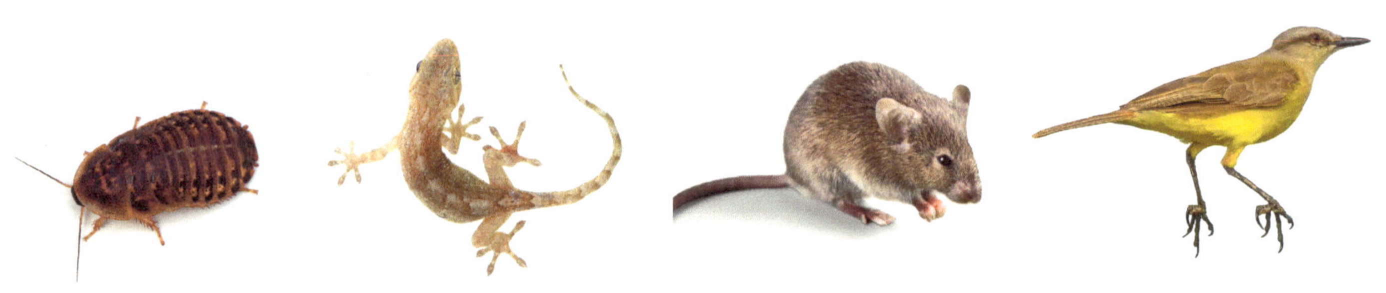

I am one of the biggest frogs in the world. I can grow up to 10 inches. That's bigger than this book!

I am very good at hiding and waiting for something
yummy to come nearby. I can sit with only my
nose and eyes sticking out of the ground or water
for a long time.
Can you hide like me?

My name is Glenda. I am a glass frog.

I live in the forests of Central and South America.
It is warm and humid here.

I am light green with spots. I have large eyes to help me see in the dark. I can grow up to 1 ½ inches.

I like to eat small insects, like ants, flies, and spiders.

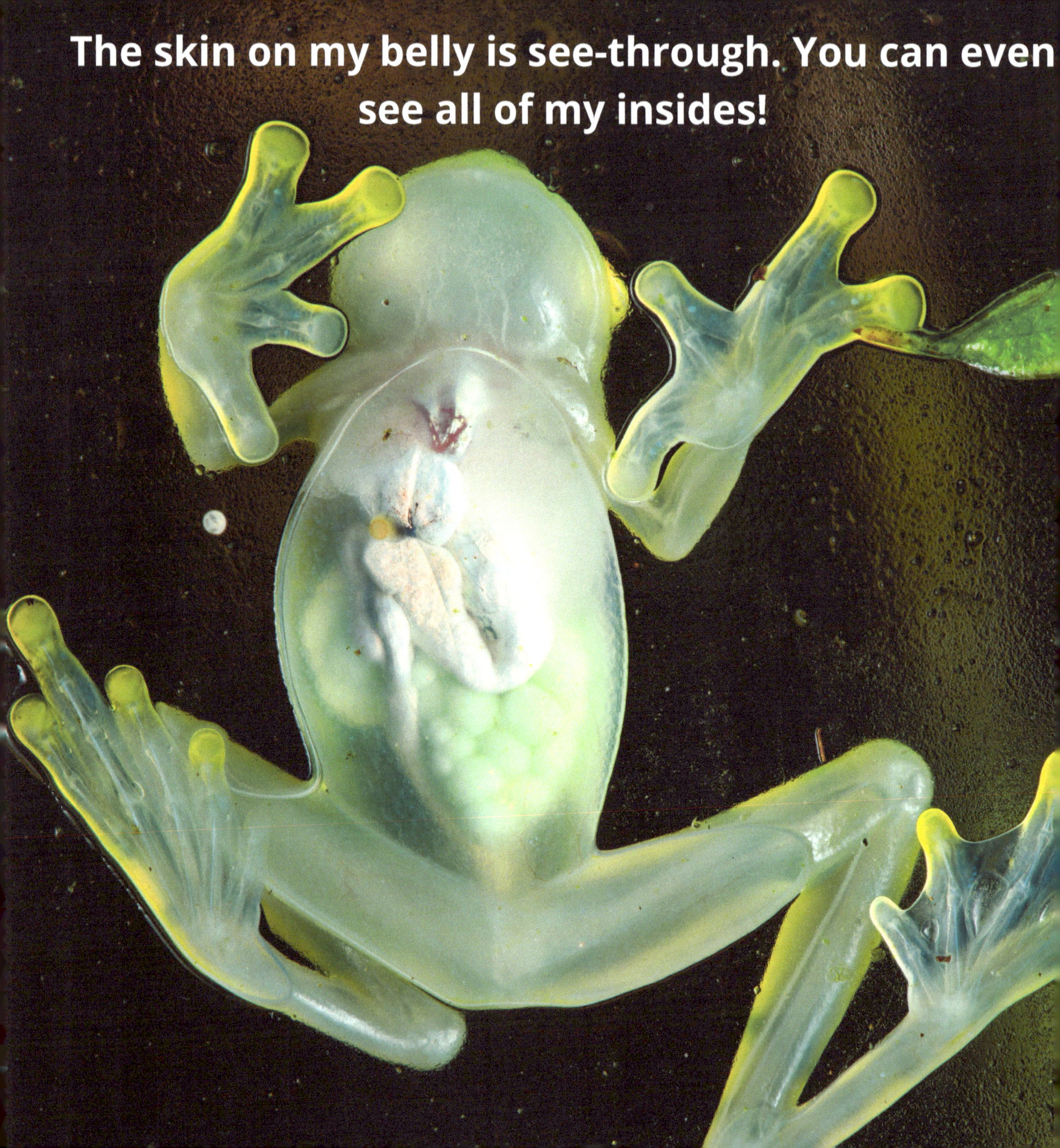

The skin on my belly is see-through. You can even see all of my insides!

My babies are born from eggs that are laid on the bottoms of leaves. After they are laid, I watch over them to make sure they are healthy when they hatch.

I spend almost my entire life in the trees. I even sleep in the leaves of trees and other tall plants. Where do you like to sleep?

My name is Maurice and I am a
Vietnamese mossy frog.

I live in the forests of
northern Vietnam
and China. I like to
live in flooded caves
and mountain
streams.

I am green and brown in color with black spots. My skin is very bumpy. I can get up to 3 ½ inches long.

I like to eat insects like beetles, crickets, and spiders.

My coloring and bumpy skin help me to blend in and look like a clump of moss. This helps me to hide from predators.

Even though I am small, I have a very loud call
that sounds like a hoot.
Can you make a call that sounds like a hoot?

My name is Dash and I am a poison dart frog.

I live in the tropical forests of Central and South America. It is very wet and warm where I live.

I can be almost any color in the rainbow. I am very small, and only grow up to 1 ½ inches.

I like to eat very small insects, like ants, termites, beetles, and fruit flies.

Some of the insects I eat cause me to give off a poison through my skin.

The people where I live used to rub their darts on my back before hunting. That is how I got my name

After my babies hatch from their eggs, I carry them
on my back to water where they can grow up.

I use my bright colors to tell predators
to stay away.
What is your favorite color?

What was your
favorite frog?